The Star-Spangled Banner

by Marcia Amidon Lusted

PEBBLE
a capstone imprint

First Facts are published by Pebble
1710 Roe Crest Drive, North Mankato, Minnesota 56003.
www.mycapstone.com

Library of Congress Cataloging-in-Publication Data
Names: Lusted, Marcia Amidon, author
Title: The Star-Spangled Banner / by Marcia Amidon Lusted.
Description: North Mankato, Minnesota : Pebble, a Capstone imprint, 2020. |
Series: First Facts. Shaping the United States of America | Audience: Grade K–3. |
Audience: Ages 6–8. Identifiers: LCCN 2019004130| ISBN 9781977108449 (hardcover)
ISBN 9781977110138 (pbk.) | ISBN 9781977108623 (ebook pdf)
Subjects: LCSH: Baltimore, Battle of, Baltimore, Md., 1814—Juvenile literature. |
Star-spangled banner (Song)—Juvenile literature. | Key, Francis Scott, 1779–1843—
Juvenile literature. | United States—History—War of 1812—Flags—Juvenile literature. |
Flags—United States—History—19th century—Juvenile literature.
Classification: LCC E356.B2 L87 2019 | DDC 784.7/1973—dc23
LC record available at https://lccn.loc.gov/2019004130

Editorial Credits
Alesha Sullivan, editor; Elyse White, designer; Jo Miller, media researcher;
Katy LaVigne, production specialist

Image Credits
Alamy: ART Collection, 10, Gado Images, 13; Granger - All Rights Reserved, Cover (bottom); News-
com: Cal Sport Media/Pat Lovell, 15, KRT, 19, UPI/Jon Soohoo, 17; North Wind Picture Archives, 7, 8;
Shutterstock: AXL, 16, Everett Historical, 9, sirtravelalot, 20; The New York Public Library/I. N. Phelps
Stokes Collection of American Historical Prints, 5; Wikimedia: Public
Domain, Cover (top), 11, 12

Design Elements
Shutterstock: Scisetti Alfio

All internet sites appearing in back matter were available and accurate
when this book was sent to press.

Printed in the United States of America.
002895

Table of Contents

Chapter 1

Bombs Bursting in Air

Rockets and bombs rained down on **Fort** McHenry. The British were attacking the American fort from their ships. A man named Francis Scott Key was watching the bombs explode. He wrote a few words on the back of a letter.

One day every American would know these words. They are the words of "The Star-Spangled Banner."

British ships attacked Fort McHenry in 1814. The fort was located near the Baltimore Harbor in Baltimore, Maryland.

fort—a building that is well defended against attacks

In the early 1800s, Great Britain was at war with France. The Americans were **trading** with the French. This upset the British. The result was the War of 1812 between the United States and Great Britain.

trade—the buying and selling of goods

The British set fire to the President's House during the War of 1812. Today this building is known as the White House.

Chapter 2

A Victory and a Poem

On September 13, 1814, Francis Scott Key was watching the battle at Fort McHenry in Maryland from a nearby ship. The British **bombarded** the Americans for hours.

Key thought America was going to lose the fight. But early the next morning, he could still see the American flag. It was flying over the fort.

Francis Scott Key woke up on September 14, 1814, and saw the American flag flying over Fort McHenry.

bombard—to attack a person or place with heavy objects or gunfire

Francis Scott Key

Key wrote a poem about the American **victory**. He called the poem "Defence of Fort M'Henry." The poem was set to music. It became a song called "The Star-Spangled Banner."

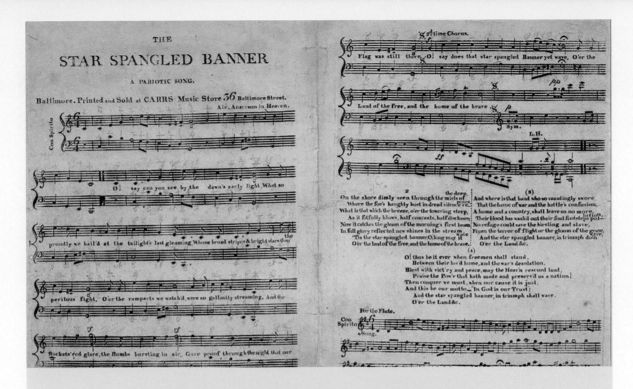

From Poem to Song

Francis Scott Key wrote "Defence of Fort M'Henry" with the idea that it would be a song. He thought about a popular song written by a British **composer**. It was called "To Anacreon in Heaven." Key wrote his words to match this tune.

composer—the writer of a piece of music

victory—a win in a fight or contest

Chapter 3

Spreading the Word

A printer in Baltimore quickly made copies of the song. It was printed in newspapers all over the city. Soon the whole nation knew the words to "The Star-Spangled Banner."

THE STAR SPANGLED BANNER.

O! say can you see by the dawn's early light,
    What so proudly we hailed at the twilights last gleaming,
Whose broad stripes and bright stars through the perilous fight,
    O'er the ramparts we watch'd were so gallantly streaming,
And the rocket's red glare, and the bomb's bursting in air,
Gave proof through the night that our flag was still there:
    Oh! say, does the star-spangled banner yet wave,
    O'er the land of the free and the home of the brave?

On the shore dimly seen through the mists of the deep,
    Where the foes haughty host in dread silence reposes,
What is that which the breeze o'er the towering steep,
    As it fitfully blows, half conceals, half discloses?
Now it catches the gleam of the morning's first beam,
In full glory reflected, now shines on the stream;
    'Tis the star-spangled banner, O, long may it wave,
    O'er the land of the free, and the home of the brave.

And where is that band who so vauntingly swore,
    That the havoc of war and the battle's confusion,
A home and a country should leave us no more?
    Their blood has washed out their foul footsteps pollution.
No refuge could save the hireling and slave
From the terror of flight, or the gloom of the grave,
    And the star-spangled banner in triumph doth wave,
    O'er the land of the free, and the home of the brave.

O! thus be it ever, when freemen shall stand,
    Between their loved home and the war's desolation,
Blessed with victory and peace, may the Heaven rescued land,
    Praise the power that hath made and preserved us a nation.
Then conquer we must, when our cause it is just,
And this be our motto—"In God is our Trust!"
    And the star-spangled banner in triumph shall wave,
    O'er the land of the free, and the home of the brave.

"The Star-Spangled Banner" was printed in Baltimore in 1814. It quickly spread to cities along the East Coast.

Fact:

Francis Scott Key's original poem is very long. It has four **stanzas.** Each stanza has eight lines. Today only the first stanza of "The Star-Spangled Banner" is sung.

stanza—a group of related lines in a poem that make up one section within the poem

"The Star-Spangled Banner" was becoming a symbol of **unity**. Throughout the 1800s it was played at many events. In 1889 the United States Navy chose "The Star-Spangled Banner" as its official song to play during the raising of the American flag.

In 1916 President Woodrow Wilson made the song even more popular. He signed an order stating "The Star-Spangled Banner" was the official national **anthem** for the U.S. armed forces.

anthem—a song of gladness or praise

unity—being together as one

Baseball and "The Star-Spangled Banner"

"The Star-Spangled Banner" was first played at a sporting event in 1918 at the World Series. American soldiers were fighting overseas in France. The song's words reminded Americans to be thankful for our military and our freedoms. Later during World War II (1939–1945), the anthem was played before every pro baseball game in America. Today this tradition continues at baseball games and other sporting events.

Chapter 4

An American Symbol

Americans were pushing to make the song the country's national anthem. Finally after dozens of **bills** were sent to the president, it was official.

On March 3, 1931, President Herbert Hoover signed a law. The law said "The Star-Spangled Banner" was to be the official national anthem of the United States of America.

It took more than two years and 40 bills to finally pass a law for "The Star-Spangled Banner" to become America's national anthem.

bill—a written idea for a new law

The flag that inspired Francis Scott Key still exists today. It is huge! The flag measures 30 feet (9 meters) long and 42 feet (13 m) wide. That's about half the size of a tennis court.

Back then, the flag had 15 stars and 15 stripes. Each state had a star and stripe. Now the American flag has 50 stars, one for each state of the United States of America.

The flag from the War of 1812 is on display at the National Museum of American History in Washington, D.C.

People often put a hand on their chest when they hear the national anthem.

"The Star-Spangled Banner" is an important reminder of America's **independence**. People stand when they hear the anthem. They think about the flag and the United States.

independence—freedom from the control of other people or things

Glossary

anthem (AN-thuhm)—a national song

bill (BIL)—a written idea for a new law

bombard (bom-BAHRD)—to attack a person or place with heavy objects or gunfire

composer (kuhm-POH-zer)—the writer of a piece of music

fort (FORT)—a place built to be strong to keep the people living there safe from attack

independence (in-di-PEN-duhnss)—freedom from the control of other people or things

stanza (STAN-zuh)—a group of related lines in a poem that make up one section within the poem

trade (TRADE)—the buying and selling of goods

unity (YOO-ni-tee)—being together as one

victory (VIK-tur-ee)—a win in a fight or contest

Read More

Kallio, Jamie. *12 Questions About "The Star-Spangled Banner."* Examining Primary Sources. Mankato, MN: 12-Story Library, 2017.

Nelson, Maria. *The National Anthem.* Symbols of America. New York: Gareth Stevens, 2015.

Troupe, Thomas Kingsley. *Birth of the Star-Spangled Banner: A Fly on the Wall History.* North Mankato, MN: Picture Window Books, 2018.

Internet Sites

The Star-Spangled Banner
https://amhistory.si.edu/starspangledbanner/

Star-Spangled Banner: 1814
https://bensguide.gpo.gov/j-star-spangled

Critical Thinking Questions

1. Look at the poem on page 13. In your own words, describe what Francis Scott Key might have been seeing that helped influence his poem.

2. Why do you think it is important for a country to have a national anthem?

3. What other symbols of the United States can you think of?

Index